uniquely
NORMAL
MANUAL

Using the Bernstein Cognitive
Method for Autism

Robert J. Bernstein

UNIQUELY NORMAL MANUAL

All marketing and publishing rights guaranteed to and reserved by:

(817) 277-0727
(817) 277-2270 (fax)
E-mail: info@fhautism.com
www.fhautism.com

ISBN: 9781949177978

ADVANCE PRAISE FOR
THE *UNIQUELY NORMAL MANUAL*

"For many parents, teacher professionals in allied fields, and others supporting autistic children (and adults, too), autism can be very challenging to understand. In response to this challenge, Rob Bernstein shares his insights and strategies for better mutual understanding through an approach based not on pressuring autistic children (and adults) to conform to school, family, and social rules, but rather employing strength-based exploration on how their minds work and what they are interested in.

Part of the beauty of Bernstein's method is its simplicity: it evaluates and works with children in their everyday environments, focusing on and doing the things that captivate the child's attention, and capitalizes on their natural absorption in those moments to teach language and social skills by creating associations between words and experiences. Departing from the traditional behavioral approach to working with children with autism, Bernstein's method seeks to understand and modify thinking processes to support closing developmental gaps via his cognitive approach based on how children process information and their developmental needs.

The ultimate goal of the method is to help children function more easily and flexibly, with less stress and frustration, in settings they will encounter throughout their lifespan. Drawing on his more than 40 years as an educational consultant and therapist for children with autism, Bernstein presents a series of case studies and practical exercises to help children develop three primary skills: logical thinking, connecting with others through language, and flexible behaviors. The manual outlines approaches to remediate specific processing issues such as tangential thinking, resisting outside structure, and difficulty considering other people's viewpoints. The exercises and the eight cases included will be of interest to all who work with or live with children with autism.

This book provides a viewpoint into the internal world of autistic children, illuminating how they think, what needs buttressing in their development, and how to provide these supports. Finally, adults may find this book helpful in reframing their childhood experiences and as a guide to better understanding of their own lives."

— Stephen Shore, Ed.D., Assistant Professor of Special Education at Adelphi University, international lecturer and consultant, author of *Beyond the Wall: Personal Experiences with Autism and Asperger Syndrome* and *Understanding Autism for Dummies*

"Robert Bernstein is one of the smartest, most people-perceptive people I know. As an educator, he has written this guide full of creative ways to stimulate language and thinking among autistic kids."

— Will Shortz, crossword editor, *The New York Times*

"Rob Bernstein's approach promotes the kind of change that enhances children because it's organic and helps them develop from inside rather than from external pressure. What I think is also critical to understand is there is a context for this work: Rob creates a safe space for a child to grow. It's more than acceptance; he joins the child's experience and is wholly nonjudgmental. It's critical to ask ourselves if we're sending double messages about our attitudes, and if the child has a safe place to take risks and change."

— Marcia Eckerd, Ph.D., clinical psychologist, Connecticut ASD Advisory Council, Board of Directors of NeuroClastic.org, author and speaker

"As a parent of an autistic child, I have first-hand benefited from Rob's method as described in *Uniquely Normal*. This manual would be an added resource for parents to practice the wisdom that Rob has shared for over three decades."

— V. R. Ferose, Senior Vice President and Head of SAP Engineering Academy, founder of the India Inclusion Foundation (IIF)

"Rob Bernstein's manual is definitely a much-needed compass for navigating a world that is not always sensory-friendly or catered to the ease of the neurodiverse population. There is no such thing as 'normal,' and the only thing that should be considered as 'abnormal' is treating others with contempt who are not allowed to have much of a fighting chance!"

— Jesse A. Saperstein, author of *Atypical* and *Getting a Life with Asperger's*

"At the age of 17 my son was crying from loneliness. He had an IEP since the age of 3, and I had spent 15 years trying to get the school to help my son to develop meaningful social connections, to no avail. All the activities I signed him up for failed to result in any connections. I spent countless rides to school giving examples of ice breakers and one-liners. It didn't work.

What I discovered after we began working with Robert Bernstein was not just that my son didn't have a friend, but that he rarely even spoke to or had any interactions with his peers despite spending 40 hours a week among kids his own age.

I was heartbroken. I can only imagine the pain my funny and kind son endured during those years of isolation.

Rob Bernstein's approach Rob purposely set up situations, using what was going on in my son's life and also his interests. including as well as his interests. In a very short time my son was asking me for advice on meeting other kids and even navigating interactions with girls!

Through working with Rob, my son has gained the skills he needed to become approachable to his peers and the confidence he needed to start interacting regularly with others.

For example, at my son's high school graduation, he spotted a classmate that he hung out with a few times on the weekends outside of school, a huge accomplishment in itself. They gave each other a classic dude embrace and said their goodbyes. It was a moment I will never forget. This was made possible by following Rob Bernstein's method.

With Rob's guidance, my son is moving into his college dorm this week, with a roommate that he has been communicating with for months.

Interestingly, the college my son is attending has a program to support students similar to my son. We discovered that none of the students in the program have a roommate, they are all opting to use the available accommodation to live in a single room, which is an amazing opportunity for those who truly need it.

If not for Rob Bernstein's method, my son would have missed out on this important milestone of having a roommate in college! I can only imagine the social interactions my son would have had when he was 4 or 5 if we had met Rob Bernstein earlier."

— Rose M. Harper, Esq.

DEDICATION

I would like to dedicate this manual to my teachers:

A.O. Ross, Professor of Psychology at Stony Brook University, gave me weekly individual sessions on the behavioral approach to education. After four years of psychology and education courses, almost all of which had a behavioral bent, I really understood behaviorism.

Aaron Lipton, Professor of Education at Stony Brook University, was an acclaimed humanist who gave me weekly individual sessions on the progressive approach to education (an approach in which the teacher guides the child based on the child's interests and motivations).

Lois Bloom, Professor of Developmental Psychology at Teachers College Columbia University, taught me in remarkable detail the normal development of a child's language. She pioneered the roles of cognition, emotion, and social behavior in language acquisition. Years later, I used her book *The Transition from Infancy to Language: Acquiring the Power of Expression* with her protocol for language development in typical children and applied it to language development in children with special needs. This was the start of my method, which fosters language development in children on the autism spectrum.

I. Ignacy Goldberg, Professor of Special Education at Teachers College Columbia University, is an internationally recognized master in the field of the Intellectually Disabled. Professor Goldberg recognized my passion for education the very first time we met, and he became my mentor. He helped me create the springboard from which I launched my own path in education, and he read my manuscript, which ultimately became *Uniquely Normal: Tapping the Reservoir of Normalcy to Treat Autism*.

CONTENTS

Foreword xi

Introduction. xv

EXERCISES AND ACTIVITIES FOR THINKING AND ORGANIZING THOUGHTS. 1

Candle and beaker: Thinking about cause and effect. 2

Rings on a post: Self-correction; big and small. 4

Helium balloons: Solving a problem together; planning; sequential thinking; expressing choices. 6

Magic tricks: Organizing thinking; verbal self-direction; verbal expression. 8

EXERCISES AND ACTIVITIES FOR ELICITING AND ORGANIZING LANGUAGE. 11

Put words into the child's mind. 13

Have the child fill in words as you read aloud 15

Have the child fill in words as you speak. 16

Have the child fill in words as you sing, and sing with the child 17

CONTENTS

Use movement to elicit language 19

Therapeutic car ride 20

EXERCISES AND ACTIVITIES DEVELOPING FLEXIBILITY. 23

Seeing things from another person's point of view 24

Overcoming perseveration 29

Waiting to take turns 31

Overcoming inflexibility in highly verbal children/young adults 33

Conclusion 37

Acknowledgments 43

About the Author 45

FOREWORD

This manual follows the mantra: *"Let the child lead, and when they do, be ready to follow."* Putting the child at the center of all our communication isn't news; it's been around for a very long time. But somehow we forget that children need to be listened to as well. This manual isn't saying to leave direction behind and give the child anything they want! It's specifically aiming for respectful communication with children on the autism spectrum.

At the heart of being autistic is the monotropic brain.* This is the reason autistic individuals struggle with change, inflexibility, being very literal, and so on. At times we feel things too much, and at other times we don't connect to them at all. This manual helps build understanding of autism and offers many examples of ways to connect, while valuing the child and the communication.

In our daily lives, concepts, and context, offer clues to a conversation and also "what's what and who's who." But noticing these things, reading faces and body language, and working out what comes first, then next, and so on, are very difficult for a person with autism to understand. As autistic individuals, we don't shift attention quickly and can get into a state of "flow" with things that capture our interest. For non-autistic people (allistic or neurotypical), dividing attention enables them to switch attention quickly. This allows for an easier connection from self to other for social interaction. Communication between self and others happens well when we can notice others and appreciate that they are separate from ourselves. This handy guide gives ideas about ways to work with autism, not against it.

Sometimes such difficulties in these areas can be misinterpreted as poor theory of mind. But this is usually not the case. Both *object permanence* (the knowledge that objects, people, emotions, etc.

---

* A monotropic mind is one that focuses its attention on a small number of interests at any time, tending to miss things outside of this attention tunnel.

continue to exist, even when out of sight) and *interoception*, one's inner senses (e.g., temperature, hunger, pain, anxiety, desire, mood change), require a person to attend to multiple stimuli in order to appreciate concepts such as "here, gone, still here but unseen, hungry, and so on." *It is our interoceptive self that allows us to connect and self-regulate our moods and emotions.* This connection also aids connection to others, so we learn how to appreciate their emotive states and live appropriately in a social system.

Too often these aspects of how autism impacts us are not understood and are judged as us being naughty, difficult, or lacking in empathy. But this is unlikely to be the case. It's more likely we haven't connected to an understanding because either we haven't noticed or we don't have the tools to respond.

This manual will help you build the right tools to communicate with your autistic child and help the child communicate with you.

It's so important to recognize these domains (object permanence and interoception) as being present in an autistic person's life. Concepts related to "poor object permanence," "poor or under-developed interoception," and the need to work and/or relate according to the person's interest are far too often overlooked.

Rob's manual, however, gives an explanation of these and examples of how to work with your child to enable them to connect.

Another aspect of our being autistic is our external sensory system (seeing, hearing, smelling, touching, tasting, knowing where we are in time and space, and being able to stay upright). In autism these senses are particularly tuned to our monotropic brains and our developing personalities. This might mean that our sensory system is quickly overloaded, or it might mean difficulties with sensory "feeling" so that we become sensory seekers. Knowing our child/ren is so important, and conducting a sensory profile so we can support them is vital. For a child, covering their ears with their hands might look odd, but it's a useful way to cope with sound sensitivity if there are no alternatives. Knowing what sensory experiences the child is having helps us support them appropriately.

This manual helps us work with the child and build a relationship. Relationships are central to our human needs, and they enable connection like nothing else does. Joining a child where they "live" and gaining permission to share in their interests will go a long way to helping them understand such things as "turn taking"—yours, mine, ours and so on. We are not brilliant in generalizing our learnings, so these processes need to be constantly practiced. As Rob writes, don't wait for an opportunity to present itself, make it happen.

— Dr. Wenn Lawson, Ph.D.
Author of *The Autistic Trans Guide to Life*

For more information, visit:
- https://www.lifescienceglobal.com/pms/index.php/jiddt/article/view/4562
- https://www.education.sa.gov.au/sites/default/files/object-permanence-interoception-and-theory-of-mind-supporting-document.pdf
- https://sparkforautism.org/discover/tags/special-interests/
- www.wennlawson.com

INTRODUCTION

The purpose of this manual is to guide you in using the Bernstein Cognitive Method for Autism (BCMA, or Bernstein Method for short). It is intended as a companion guide to *Uniquely Normal: Tapping the Reservoir of Normalcy to Treat Autism** and works hand-in-hand with the twenty-seven client stories in that book. It speaks primarily to parents, but teachers, therapists, and others who work with children with autism will find it useful.

There is nothing in my method that should surprise you or seem out of the ordinary. One parent told me, "This is a common-sense approach," because it uses everyday situations to help children with autism progress with language, socialization, and organization. You don't need a graduate school education to use this method; you have all the knowledge and skills you need. You already know how to do everything necessary to make a difference for your child.

If you're like most people, though, you need to learn how to apply these skills in a timely, systematic, and deliberate manner to create change—sometimes transformational change—in your child. In her foreword to my book, Dr. Temple Grandin emphasized the natural practicality of my techniques. Still, many of us need to modify our habits to help us recognize, capture, and process precious educational moments when they occur.

Perhaps the most important principle in my approach is that people are happiest and most open to change when they are absorbed in their actions. In these moments, action and learning become effortless. Most toddlers don't struggle when learning to walk or talk or interact with other children. Normal development feels automatic and inevitable: when you were little, you naturally pulled yourself up to your feet, spoke the language the adults around

---

* By Robert J. Bernstein with Robin Cantor-Cooke (Arlington, TX: Future Horizons, 2017).

you were speaking, and became comfortable with the people most familiar to you. You weren't aware that you were learning; you were focused on the challenge and fun of these new activities. It happens in adulthood, too: moments when we're lost in the pleasure of what we're doing, unaware of time, place, and everything except what we're involved in. Psychologist Mihaly Csikszentmihalyi describes these as episodes of optimal experience, characterized by deep engagement between our inner and outer states of being—what he calls *flow*.* It's the same for people with autism: they are happiest and most open to growth and change when they are absorbed in their actions.

Unfortunately, the natural rhythm of development skips a beat in many people with autism. In this manual, I suggest ways you can help them recover that beat by fostering their engagement with their surroundings. My technique comprises both natural, real-life situations you can exploit and organically grown exercises you can introduce to encourage moments of flow. (The technique is useful for both children and adults, but, as most readers will be dealing with young people on the spectrum, I'll be referring more to children than to adults in the pages that follow.)

My working definition of flow is to either use a naturally occurring real-life activity that involves language or create such an activity to capture and exploit moments of optimal experience. Both options enhance learning by inserting verbal interactions into moments of deep engagement and helping children create connections between words and their experiences. The first option involves using a situation

---

* For more, see *Flow: The Psychology of Optimum Experience* (New York: Harper Perennial, 1991) and *Finding Flow: The Psychology of Engagement with Everyday Life* (New York: Basic Books, 1997), both by Csikszentmihalyi.

that you find yourself in—a trip to the zoo, visiting Grandma, opening the refrigerator—and applying techniques to exploit your child's moments of flow. The second option involves setting up situations designed to engage your child and create moments of flow, and using the sample dialogues in this manual to address the child's needs.

My intention is for you to capture perhaps one educational moment each day that is perfectly suited to your child, and pursue it as long as the child allows the flow to continue. How long is that? It depends on the moment and the child. My session with six-year-old Jackie at a park in upstate New York is a good example.

Jackie ran to the swings, chose one, sat down, and looked at me expectantly. It was clear that he wanted me to push him. I looked right at him and said, "Push me." He didn't respond, so I continued with "Push," "Push the swing," "Push me up," and any other variation I could think of to get him to verbalize what he wanted to happen. Still no response. I then stepped behind Jackie, pushed gently, and, when the swing returned, stopped it for a moment as I spoke some variation of "Push me" again. I then released the swing with a gentle thrust and repeated the process. Every time he heard my words, he let out a yell, trying to speak. I must have pushed the swing, stopped it, called out one of my "Push me" variations, and heard Jackie's squawking response at least fifty times. At no point was I certain of the outcome, but I kept going. Who was I to deny Jackie the chance to speak when he was trying so hard? I would have done it 100 times or 500 times, as long as he kept trying to speak. Then, after a stream of yelps, he pursed his lips and spat out a resounding "Puh!" That was it! In that moment, Jackie's mind connected action to language. The logjam was broken. That day at the park, he said his first three words: push, dog, and water.

Parents ask me all the time how long they should continue doing an exercise. The answer is that it depends on how the child responds. Every child is different. Tune into yours. Even if your child doesn't seem to be responding, give yourself at least fifteen minutes to pursue the exercise. Yes, fifteen minutes can feel like forever when you're repeating yourself and getting little or no response. But think about Jackie: if your six-year-old kid had never spoken a word in his life and one day erupted into language, how much of your time would that be worth—an hour? Ten hours? A hundred?

How about a quarter of an hour?

I'm asking you to spend fifteen minutes of intensive intervention each day doing what I call the perfect exercise, one that might catapult your child to the next level. It may take many repetitions and variations, and intentional focus on how your child responds. Or doesn't respond: sometimes we think a child is oblivious to what we're doing because they're not responding in the way we'd envisioned. But an unexpected response, or even no perceptible response, may still predict a great leap. Imagine if I had ended the swing exercise after thirty repetitions instead of fifty. That day would have been pretty much the same as the day before, and Jackie probably would not have uttered a word.

These exercises are not the same thing as having fun with your child: you're playing different roles, and your experiences will differ. The exercises may be flow-like for the child, but for you they'll require energy and discipline and may feel intense. Remember, we're dealing with a moving target: your goals are likely to change after every activity, and you can't predict what the changes will be.

One goal that does not change: to witness something remarkable every time you share one of these encounters with your child. The remarkable thing may be observing something new about how the child thinks or seeing the child grow in a way you didn't expect. Increments of growth, however small, matter: when our kids are not progressing, they fall more and more behind as they get older. The idea is for the child to continue to progress, to acquire skills and develop sensibilities that help them function in the neurotypical world. Ensuring the progress of kids with special needs was the idea behind the Individuals with Disabilities Education Act (IDEA), a provision of which was the development of an individualized education program (IEP) for every special needs kid enrolled in public school. While some parents and education professionals have criticized IEPs for being more concerned with procedure than with results,* I think an IEP is fine as long as the lesson plan for tomorrow builds on the child's experience *today*. For me, there is excitement in anticipating what a client might accomplish during a session because I am always challenging the child to do more than he or she did last time. As your child ascends to higher levels of development, you will feel the same thrill.

The Bernstein Method offers a cognitive, developmental perspective on perceiving and understanding the child's needs, and determining what types of interventions can facilitate growth. Children, adolescents, and adults with autism cannot help but be where they are developmentally. It is our mission to help them advance to the next level as naturally as possible.

To get the most out of this manual and *Uniquely Normal*, I ask you to have an open mind. If you are anything like the thousands of people I have trained to work with children on the spectrum, you may need to let go of many of the precepts you've learned and

---

* Audrey McCray Sorrels, Herbert J. Rieth, and Paul T. Sindelar, *Critical Issues in Special Education: Access, Diversity, and Accountability* (London: Pearson, 2003).

habits you've formed. It's hard to escape our training, even if we're not using it consciously. I was once administering a test called the Autism Diagnostic Observation Schedule (ADOS) to a five-year-old. During one of the play exercises, she was having a pretend birthday party and making pizza. I asked her what she wanted to drink. I expected that she would say something like "Coke" or "soda." When I was growing up, a slice of pizza and a soda cost twenty-five cents (yes, we're talking ancient times here). To this day, that would be my favorite drink with pizza, but it's taboo for most health-conscious people, including myself. When this child told me she wanted water with her pizza, I realized that I had been brainwashed to crave Coke with mine. It must have been all those commercials I sat through when I was a kid.

What I'm asking you do to is to break the habit of Coke and pizza, or burger and fries, or whatever behaviors you believe you must do to nurture your child's progress. This feels somewhere between hard and impossible because almost all of us were raised in a behavioral system. "Do your homework before you go out to play" probably sounds as natural to you as Coke and pizza sounds to me. This behavioral approach, known as the Premack principle and based on the research of David Premack, stipulates that people will agree to do something they dislike if doing so will enable them to do something they do like. Thus, we require children to earn the right to do something they enjoy by requiring them to first attend to their responsibilities. This is fine for neurotypical children, but I believe that behavioral approaches don't work for kids on the autism spectrum and could even do them harm. Behavioral techniques rely on repetition—getting a barely verbal child to say *please* five times before giving her a snack, for example—which reinforces the repetitive tendencies of kids with autism. You end up teaching this child the falsehood that rote repetition of a word will get her needs met. Also, training kids with autism to behave more like neurotypical kids doesn't help them learn to navigate the neurotypical world; it merely makes them appear less eccentric. I'm not concerned with how these kids look to others; my concern is understanding why they are the way they are and engaging them in a way that exploits their cognitive potential and capacity to connect with other people.

Traditional educational approaches work for most of us but less so for people who think differently. For example, many of us learned addition and subtraction by first counting to 10. We played with the numbers and figured out that if 3 + 7 = 10, then 10 - 7 = 3. In doing this, we unwittingly absorbed the idea that if you put two numbers together to create a bigger one and you take one of those numbers away, you get the smaller number again. But kids on the autism spectrum, whose thinking may be more linear and less flexible, need to be explicitly taught the reversibility concept to fully understand addition and subtraction. In the same way you need to grasp the concept of *big* to grasp *small*, and understand *on* to understand *off*, kids with autism need to understand the reciprocal relationship between adding and subtracting.

So, as you use this manual, intensify your focus on your child's behaviors. Tune in and see if there are breakthroughs in the child's thinking, vocalizations, use of language, ways of relating to others, and cognitive flexibility. Educating kids on the autism spectrum requires more energy and discipline than you might expect. They do not learn the way neurotypical children do, and they cannot be taught the same way we were taught. The exercises will probably take more out of you than they take out of your child, but they are well worth the effort.

The methods you'll learn have three key components, which are to:

1. *Identify a moment when the child is engaged, or create a situation where the child is likely to become engaged.* Exploiting these episodes of optimal experience will be as rewarding to the most severely autistic child as to the most advanced Asperger genius.

2. *Recognize which situations might make a difference to your child and use them to reach the next level of development.* When your son utters his first word, he may soon put two words together. Your daughter's first interaction with another child may lead to her first friendship. When you see even the slightest glimmer of progress in your child, take note of the situation that fostered it and devise ways to repeat or recreate it.

3. *Understand the multilevel significance of your child's responses and behaviors.* Progress seldom happens in a linear way. A small step forward might spark a seemingly unconnected yet profound developmental leap days or weeks later. Cultivate patience as you work with your child, and trust that the process will yield results.

The goal of all these exercises is to insert verbal communication into a moment of flow, which insinuates language into the child's experience in a natural feeling way. This is as important for verbal children as it is for nonspeaking ones: the better children can express themselves in language, the more likely they are to effectively connect with the neurotypical world. When kids on the spectrum grasp that they can use words to propel what's inside them out into the open, they begin to catch up to their peers. This is especially true for young children, in whom the language part of the brain is still developing and whose brains are most flexible. My method tunes into children's natural and sometimes automatic behaviors and instills a cognitive pattern that makes their lives easier, more connected, and more independent.

One issue throughout the life of someone on the autism spectrum is feeling like an outsider much, if not all, of the time. The purpose of societal institutions—school, work, social events, religious gatherings, community functions—is to coax people to fit into prescribed norms, and people on the spectrum seldom do. School systems, standardized tests, and criteria for deciding whom to place in special education classes are typically geared toward identifying what the child is lacking. These systems are based on a deficit model, which was in turn fashioned upon the medical model, which espouses the traditional behavioral approach for educating kids on the autism spectrum. Which is to say, it focuses on trying to modify the behaviors of kids with autism rather than trying to modify the ways they think. A major problem with the deficit-based approach is that it intervenes after a child has developed problems at school. The Bernstein method intervenes to prevent problems in the first place.

A method that has something in common with mine is naturalistic developmental behavioral interventions (NDBI), pioneered by Laura Schreibman and her colleagues at University of California San Diego. NDBI highlights attributes of cognitive development, such as joint attention (the ability to share interest with another person in an object or activity) and participation (joining in an activity rather than sitting passively on the sidelines). The NDBI method also resembles mine in that it leans away from arbitrary and artificial response-reward protocols, such as rewarding a child with a lollipop because they hung up their coat. But unlike my method, NDBI combines its focus on developmental growth with behavior-based interventions, as exemplified by the applied behavior analytic (ABA) method. This veers away from my method because it takes a behavioral approach to early language development, emphasizing imitation and achieving established, objective goals. My method takes an integrative approach, following the lead of the child and paralleling normal language development. Still, despite some differences, both the NDBI method and mine are built upon a theoretical and practical framework.

In creating the Bernstein method, I have used theoretical knowledge to create practical, real-life activities, exercises, and interventions to help kids on the spectrum flourish and grow. This manual concentrates on three of their greatest challenges: thinking in an organized, logical way; using language to connect with others; and dismantling rigid behaviors in favor of flexible ones. Being flexible is key to establishing healthy, genuine, mutual relationships, which often eludes people with autism. It's difficult, if not impossible, to maintain a friendship if you can't empathize with another person's point of view, and empathy often doesn't come naturally to people on the spectrum.

In addition to cognitive, language, and behavioral issues are sensory ones that affect children with autism. Being physically comfortable—feeling at home in one's body when at school, at work, or at home—is the foundation upon which any approach to autism is based, and this needs to be considered when implementing the Bernstein method. If a child is overwhelmed by noise in a lunchroom, stressed by bright lights in a classroom, or bothered by the tags on a gym uniform, then both the child and the school must make compromises before real learning can take place.

Let's get started.

EXERCISES AND ACTIVITIES FOR THINKING AND ORGANIZING THOUGHTS

The following exercises help children learn to think and organize their thoughts. Hearing and using standard language (contrasted with nonstandard, private ways of communicating) are fundamental to the success of these exercises. The dialogues I offer are examples of effective exchanges. They are not meant to be followed verbatim, but rather to guide you toward productive verbal interactions with your child. The variations are endless. Create your own responses, depending on what the child says moment to moment. Just focus on using standard English so your child grows accustomed to hearing how everyday conversations sound and feel. Every situation is different and every child responds uniquely, so the dialogues you and your child share will also be unique. I offer an approximate age level for each exercise, but any exercise can be used with any age child. You can also use an exercise for an older child to test your child's cognitive function.

CANDLE AND BEAKER

THINKING ABOUT CAUSE AND EFFECT.

AGE 6 and up.

MATERIALS 1000 ml. beaker; small candle. Beakers meant for chemistry experiments can be ordered online. Don't use an ordinary glass jar—it can't withstand the heat.

1. Set the candle on a heat-proof surface and light it. Ask the child, "What would happen if I covered the candle with the beaker?" If the child says the candle would go out, ask them why. Listen to the answer, and then say, "Let's see if you're right." Turn the beaker over and place it over the candle, cutting off the oxygen supply. Then affirm the child's prediction: "Yes! You were right!"

   If the child says they don't know what will happen, you might say, "All right. Let's try it and see what happens." Then place the beaker over the candle and wait for the flame to extinguish. Observe the child's reaction. Then ask the child why they think the candle went out. Listen to the child's answer and respond. You might say, "Yes, the candle went out because a flame needs oxygen to burn, and covering the candle with the beaker cut off its oxygen supply." When you use simple, logical language, you enhance the child's ability to construct coherent sentences.

2. Then engage the child with questions designed to help them grasp the concept of cause and effect. Here are some examples

of questions that will stimulate a child's ability to think logically and make logic-based predictions:

- "Why didn't the candle go out right away?"
- "If we raise the beaker an inch, what do you think will happen?"
- "Let's do it again, but this time let's put the beaker over the candle for twenty seconds and then lift it up. What do you think will happen to the candle? Why?"
- "How can we keep the candle burning, even with the beaker over it?"
- "If we raise the beaker half an inch, will the candle keep burning? Let's try it and see what happens."

RINGS ON A POST

SELF-CORRECTION; BIG AND SMALL.

AGE 4 and up.

MATERIALS The classic toy with rings on a narrowing post, or a similar toy with parts that need to be placed in order from largest to smallest. For the purposes of this exercise, the post must be flared at the bottom so that the rings fit in only one sequence.

The goals of this activity are to see whether the child has a functional understanding of big and small; provide practice placing objects in a prescribed order; and get the child to express themself in an organized way, in full sentences, and tell you how to place the rings on the post. The activity has no exact instructions: Your interaction with the child should unfold naturally as you observe their response to the toy. Speak to the child in complete sentences throughout the exercise.

Here's how to start:

1. Disassemble the toy and set it before the child with the rings spread out in no particular order. Then say, "Can you put this together?" Don't demonstrate how to arrange the rings. Instead, observe what the child does with the toy. Are they placing the rings on the post randomly, or by trial and error, or do they get the idea of finding the biggest one as they're doing the task? Do

they place the rings on the post out of order, then remove the ring that doesn't fit? Pay attention to your child's thought process as they work on the task.

2. If the child arranges the rings on the post correctly, acknowledge their success. Then remove the rings and say, "Now I'll try do it, and you tell me what I should do." If they say, "Start with the red one," ask why. Listen for whether the child verbalizes something about starting with the big, bigger, or biggest ring.

3. If the child self-corrects by removing a ring they placed out of order, then the child understands the idea of the exercise. If the child persists in arranging the rings out of order, demonstrate how to arrange the rings correctly. Then let them try again.

4. If necessary, hold up the biggest and smallest rings and ask, "Which is the big one?" and "Which is the small one?" several times. You might also point out that the larger the ring, the larger the hole in its center. If the child still doesn't grasp the concept of big and small, switch to other objects to teach it. Regular household items work well: a large can of tomato sauce next to a can of tuna; an adult's shoe next to the child's. Be playful and creative.

5. Remove the rings from the post, mix them up, and ask the child to arrange them again unaided. As they begin with a larger ring, hold up a small one and ask, "Why not this one?" The goal is to try to get the child to verbalize their reasoning: "This one is too small," or "The red one is bigger." Or arrange the rings yourself in the wrong order and ask the child to say what's awry. As the child begins to understand the task and can complete it, introduce more language in different ways.

HELIUM BALLOONS

SOLVING A PROBLEM TOGETHER; PLANNING; SEQUENTIAL THINKING; EXPRESSING CHOICES.

AGE 4 to teens.

MATERIALS Balloons, helium tank.

This activity provides fun and creative opportunities to interact with the child and promote several thinking and communication skills.

1. Give the child an inflated helium balloon. Say, "Don't let go! Don't let go!"—making it clear with your face and voice that that's exactly what you want and expect the child to do. Many children can't resist the temptation to release the balloon, but if yours holds on, take back the balloon and "accidentally" let it go.

2. When the balloon floats up to the ceiling, see if the child tracks its progress, or acts concerned, or laughs. Do they join you in the mishap by glancing at the balloon, pointing at it, or reaching for it? Observe your child's joint attention ability—in other words, their capacity to share your interest in and focus on the escaped balloon.

3. Ask the child, "Now what do we do? How do we get it down? Do you want to get a chair to stand on?" If they want to get a chair,

encourage them to verbalize what they're doing and what their plan is.

4. Say, "Stand on the chair" while keeping an eye on or arm around the child; "Are you tall enough to reach it?"; "What are we going to do?"; "Do you want me to pick you up?"; "Should I stand on the chair?"; "Should we get a stepladder?"; "Who's going to climb the stepladder?" If your ceiling is so high that recovering the balloon isn't an option, say, "Should we blow up another one?" Listen as the child answers and respond in complete sentences that keep the conversation going.

5. Ask, "Do you want a ribbon on the balloon?" Wait for the answer, then ask why or why not. If the answer is yes, ask, "How should we do this? You hold the balloon and I tie it, or I hold the balloon and you tie it?" Then, "How are we going to cut the ribbon?"

6. When you either recover the balloon or inflate another one, ask, "Should we break the balloon?" If the child says yes, ask, "How should we do it? With a needle? Do you think it will make a noise? Will it be loud?" Then, "Should we make another one?"

7. Say, "Okay, how can we make a new balloon? What do we need to do first? What's next? Tell me the all the steps." (Secure the uninflated balloon to the helium tank spigot. Turn the valve. Tie the balloon. Get the ribbon. Cut the ribbon. Hold the balloon. Tie the balloon with the ribbon.)

8. Ask, "Should we make another one for your brother (sister, mother, father, friend?)"

MAGIC TRICKS

ORGANIZING THINKING; VERBAL SELF-DIRECTION; VERBAL EXPRESSION.

AGE 7 and up.

MATERIALS Deck of playing cards.

In this activity the child will watch you perform a five-step magic trick and then learn to do it on their own. The activity works with a variety of tricks: simple sleight-of-hand tricks, disappearing coin tricks, magic wand tricks, and many others. The simpler the trick, the better the activity will work. There are many online resources for children's card tricks and lots of demonstrations on YouTube.

I like to start with this basic, pick-a-card, any-card trick in which the child picks a card from the deck and you magically know which it is. Each step of the trick is noted below. I suggest you do a dry run on your own to perfect your technique before trying it with a child (I learned this the hard way).

Start by demonstrating the trick:

1. Show the child that you are using a standard deck of cards.

2. Fan out the cards facedown in your hands and say, "Pick a card. Look at it, but don't let me see it."

3. After the child picks a card, cut the deck more or less in half and hold a pile of cards facedown in each hand.

4. Say, "Now put the card facedown on top of the pile in my right hand." Make sure they place the card on top of the pile.

5. As the child is putting the card on the pile in your right hand, pivot your left hand and glance at the card on the bottom. This is your indicator card, the card that will be on top of the one the child chose.

6. Now place the pile of cards in your left hand facedown on top of those in your right hand.

7. Say, "Now I'm going to look through the deck and find your card." Turn the deck face up and fan out the cards from left to right so that the faceup card at the top of the pile remains the right-most card in the fan. Then, find the indicator card. The child's card is the card to the right of the indicator card.

Next ask the child if they would like to learn the trick. (If they say no, I hope you have more than one trick up your sleeve!) Say, "Now you do the trick on me. Let's go through it together, and I'll explain every step."

Go through each step of the trick as numbered above, describing in complete sentences what you're doing. If the child loses track of the progression, say, "Okay, let's go back and do that step again." What you're doing is organizing in both action and language a seemingly magical occurrence, and creating a linear flow of events that culminates in a surprise and sense of mastery.

When you have gone through all the steps of the trick, hand the cards to the child so they can try doing it on you. Say, "You have to give clear instructions so I know what to do. Start by saying, "I'm mixing up the cards."

EXERCISES AND ACTIVITIES FOR ELICITING AND ORGANIZING LANGUAGE

The goal of the exercises in this section is to get the child to use words. The mechanism is to use your words to make it happen.

What I want you to do is speak to the child using words that inspire the child to find words of their own. What I don't want you to do is encourage the child to mimic what you're saying. Learning to reproduce a string of sounds doesn't help children develop their own vocabulary; it turns them into parrots who perform verbal stunts that delight the adults in the room. That's why I never praise nonspeaking children when they start to talk; to do so would be to encourage them to perform rather than communicate. What I want for my clients is what you want for your child: to enable the child to convey to other people what's happening in their inner world. The best way I've found to do this is not to suggest to kids what they should say, but rather to coax them into expressing themselves in their imperfect, unique ways.

A recent video session I had with Zach, seventeen, is a good example. I'd been working with Zach for several months during the pandemic and he'd grown accustomed to seeing me in my home office with a shelf of books behind my head. But this time I was in an unfamiliar setting: a kitchen with wooden cabinets where the books should have been. Zach noticed immediately.

"Where are you?" he asked.

"I'm in New Hampshire," I said. "My wife and I come up here every summer."

"Oh," Zach said. Then, after a pause: "What did you take?"

Now, this is a kid who's fascinated by maps and roads: highways,

11

byways, interstates—we'd had sessions where he talked about little else. I knew exactly what he meant but saw an opportunity to expand his language skills, so I played dumb.

"What did you mean by that question?" I said, hoping he'd be more specific.

"What did you take?"

He wasn't biting, so I gave an answer I knew he'd reject.

"I took a suitcase and a water bottle." He made a face. "Oh," I said, acting confused, "I guess that's not what you meant. What do you mean?"

"What did you take?"

Zach couldn't do it; he didn't have the words to express his thought.

"I just told you, I took a suitcase and—"

"Car!" he said.

Now we were getting somewhere.

"Okay, car," I said, nodding and smiling. "What did you mean?"

I was not taunting him; I was trying to get him to use a different set of words to communicate what he was thinking. Exchanging information was not the point: The point was for Zach to make himself understood. The answer had to come from him, and I was willing to persist until it happened. And then it did.

"How did you get there?" he said.

"Oh!" I said. "I took I-91 to route 89, then …"

In that small intervention, I prodded Zach to dig inside for words that would get across his meaning to another person. He came through beautifully if unwittingly; he wasn't aware of the leap he'd taken, but he didn't have to be. It happened whether he knew it or not.

PUT WORDS INTO THE CHILD'S MIND

AGE All.

The goal of this exercise is introduce language into an activity you're sharing with the child. Close attention pays off here, as you'll be trying to intuit what the child is thinking, and choosing words you think they might use to describe it.

The idea is to identify a moment when you're tuned into the child's thinking process, and voice aloud some words you imagine the child might use if they had the verbal skill to do so. If the activity lasts longer than a moment or two, go with the flow by inserting more words that feel appropriate to whatever is going on.

Here are some examples:

1. When searching for something—a jigsaw puzzle piece, perhaps—insert the words "Where?" or "Where is it?" or "Where could it be?"

2. When the child picks up a piece and moves to place it in the puzzle, block the space and say, "Move," "Move my hand," or "Move my finger."

3. When the child tosses you a ball and wants you to throw it back, say, "Throw the ball," or "I'm throwing the ball;" then, "Catch the ball."

4. When pushing a toy car back and forth with the child, say, "Go," "Push," "Push the car," "I push to you," or "Push the car to me."

5. When the child wants more of something, say, "More," "More please," "I want more," or "I would like more, please."

6. When the child wants you to continue blowing up a balloon, say, "More," "Again," "Blow again," "Blow it up again," or "Blow up the balloon again."

The best outcome is when the child gets the idea and says words that come from within themselves, rather than mimicking what they heard you say. Whether or not they reproduce the word or phrase, the goal is to help the child connect language to their thought process, and to realize that language is a way to share with others what's inside themselves. To that end, avoid repeating the same words and phrases when you do this exercise because that encourages rote speaking. All too often, kids on the spectrum are praised for mechanically repeating what they think their parents and teachers want them to say. Rote speaking is the opposite of what we want these kids to do, and it needs to be unlearned. Help your child do this by varying the combinations of words you use.

HAVE THE CHILD FILL IN WORDS AS YOU READ ALOUD

AGE All.

Many children's books feature repetitive and predictable text to provide language practice. When you're reading aloud to your child, leave out the last word or sentence of a familiar part of the story, pause to observe their reaction, and encourage them to fill in the blank. This is easier than you think. At the beginning of almost any story, you could say, "Once upon a ___ ..." and wait for the child to say "time." This exercise is particularly effective when you're reading a beloved story that the child knows well.

HAVE THE CHILD FILL IN WORDS AS YOU SPEAK

AGE All.

Come up with an idea that lends itself to conversation, put it into words, and let the child complete the statement. For example, if you feel your stomach rumble, you might say, "I haven't eaten all day. I'm so ___ ."

HAVE THE CHILD FILL IN WORDS AS YOU SING, AND SING WITH THE CHILD

AGE All.

Making music with your child, whether by singing or playing an instrument, can prove useful. A 2018 study by the University of Montreal and McGill University found that musical activities improved the communication skills and brain connectivity of children with autism, and boosted the family's quality of life.

Conversation has a lot in common with music: When conversing with another person, we need to pay attention to what they're saying, pick up on the rhythm of the exchange and understand when it's our turn to speak, and ignore irrelevant sounds and background noise. Making music also requires us to listen closely, attend to rhythm, and tune out musical parts other than our own. By singing or playing a musical instrument in turn with others, kids with autism can naturally and organically absorb communication skills. Music is a wonderful way for kids to connect with language.

Here's an example of how to share a musical activity with your child:

1. The child leads by playing an instrument—say, a guitar. The child doesn't need to have any skill on the instrument; simply brushing a hand over the strings and making a sound is enough.

2. Now you respond, picking up on the rhythm with a tambourine, small drum, or overturned cardboard box. Or you can drum your hands on a table or your lap—just responding in rhythm is enough.

3. Next, stop the music and then start up again. Play a couple of times like this.

4. Now you establish a rhythm first and see if the child can follow it. Stop and start playing as before with you leading.

5. Next, switch instruments and repeat the exercise.

My favorite instrument for this activity is a child's xylophone. If you can get hold of one and a couple of mallets, you can do the exercise with both of you playing the same instrument. Take turns playing the xylophone, duplicating the child's rhythm and, when you lead, encouraging the child to duplicate yours. If you can play a simple tune like "Mary Had a Little Lamb," see how the child follows it, if at all. Insist on taking your turn, even if it's only for a few seconds. Knowing when to remain quiet and let the other person "speak" is an important communication skill.

There are many creative variations of this activity. If you don't have a musical instrument handy, get some canned beans and a couple of spoons, and bang away. Empty plastic food storage containers also work. The goal is to get the child to interact with you through sound. It doesn't have to be beautiful to be effective.

USE MOVEMENT TO ELICIT LANGUAGE

AGE All.

Take advantage of the child's physical activities to elicit language. Getting into bed or a car or down from a ladder, chair, or windowsill; and going outside, into a store, or through a turnstile are all opportunities for your child to develop language skills. Speak in full

sentences (even one-word sentences are okay) and vary your intervening remarks. For example, when the child wants to be picked up, use phrases such as "Up, please," "I want to go up," and "Pick me up." Likewise, intervene with "I want to go down," "Down!" (while pointing), "Down please," and "Put me down" when the child wants help getting down. Children often come up with their own combinations of words when they're exposed to different ways of speaking. That's why it's necessary to vary the way you express yourself in these interventions. We all tend to fall into familiar speech patterns; use these exercises to vary yours.

It's also helpful to establish context before trying to elicit language. While you're preparing to leave the house, pose a question such as "Where do you want to go?" or "Where should we go?" This helps the child focus on what's about to happen—the two of you are going somewhere—and directs their thinking toward what they might like to do.

THERAPEUTIC CAR RIDE

AGE 3 and up.

A car ride offers lots of opportunities for verbal interactions, and one of my trusted ways of eliciting language is to take a young client out to a local ice cream parlor or pizza joint. After we get in the car, I may fiddle with the radio or my phone for a while to see if the child will tell me to put on my seatbelt or request help with theirs. One girl said, "Seatbelt on," which gave me an opening to ask, "Whose seatbelt should we put on?" A full sentence soon followed: "Put seatbelt on, Rob."

Remember, we want the child to have a dialogue with you. One way to start would be to say, "Put on your seatbelt, Amelia." Then wait. If there's no response, ask "What should I do, Amelia?" If Amelia needs more help, you might say, "Should we put your seatbelt on?" or, "Should I put my seatbelt on?" If the child says "Yes," say, "Okay. Tell me what to do." You always want to go back to the question, "What should I do?" or "What should we do?" as soon as you can.

The goal is for the child to answer the question in a full sentence. But again, be careful: you don't want to prompt a rote response, with the child locking into saying things one way—the downfall of many good intentions. You need to encourage flexibility in the child's answer so they start to comprehend the infinite variety of verbal expression. Mimicking the same set of words to please a trusted adult results in mechanical, disconnected speech. That's the opposite of what we're trying to do.

I can't emphasize enough how important it is to foster variety in both your own language and your child's. In the car scenario, Amelia's "Put seatbelt on" was a great sentence, but if she repeats it verbatim every time she gets into a car, she's merely parroting a string of words that she knows pleased me the first time she said it. It hurts me when the kids I work with speak repetitively because I know they were unwittingly taught to do it by well-meaning adults in their lives.

Our goal is to encourage our children to think logically and use words generated from within in unrehearsed, spontaneous ways. Continuing with Amelia, who is based on a real client of mine, here's an exchange in which I encourage her to take ownership not of a specific phrase but of syntax and real language:

Amelia: Put seatbelt on.

Me: And tomorrow, when Mommy drives, what will you tell Mommy?

Amelia: Mommy, put seatbelt on.

Sometimes I get the child started by varying the syntax I used earlier:

Me: And how about Daddy? Daddy, get ...

Amelia: Daddy, get your seatbelt on.

When I ask parents how their children express themselves verbally, they sometimes report that their kids ask for things by starting with "I want," which becomes, through repetition, essentially one word, as in Iwanna snack. When I ask if the child ever asks for something in a different way, for example, "Get me juice," instead of

"I want juice," the parent almost invariably says, "No, only 'I want.'" The child now needs to unlearn this rote way of speaking.

How do children learn to speak by rote? We teach them, despite our best intentions. We get drawn into the child's repetitive nature and unintentionally encourage a repetitive response. I hear it over and over again: the first time their child says "Iwanna cookie," the parents are thrilled. And, as they tell me, they don't want the child to lose the phrase, so whenever the child says "Iwanna cookie," they praise the child and reach for the Chips Ahoy. This is how the child learns to respond in a repetitive manner. What would work better would be for parents to say, "Would you like a cookie? Which kind would you like?" or "Are you in the mood for chocolate chip or oatmeal raisin?" or "Which would you prefer: a cookie or a donut?" Language comes from ideas we want to express, and each of us expresses ideas in our own way—that is, when we aren't lulled into verbal shorthand. Listen to yourself when you speak to your child: are you repeating the same phrases over and over? I'm reminded of those zippy responses my cell phone offers when a text message comes in, such as "What's up?" and "How was it?" They're convenient but pat, a way to respond without thinking. Try to resist this sort of speech when you're with your child. The more thought you put into expressing your ideas in complete, lucid sentences, the sooner your child will learn to transform ideas into language.

EXERCISES AND ACTIVITIES
DEVELOPING FLEXIBILITY

The repetitive behavior characteristic of autism is too seldom taken into consideration when flexibility is taught. Teaching people with autism to be more flexible in their thoughts and actions can significantly enhance their use of language, ability to organize their thinking, comfort in social situations, and overall functioning in the neurotypical world.

SEEING THINGS FROM ANOTHER PERSON'S POINT OF VIEW

The following scene approximates a therapeutic session I had with two boys whom I wanted to become more flexible.

Twelve-year-old Jimmy and fourteen-year-old Adam were in my office and needed to agree on where we would go for an outing. My goal was for them to come to a mutually satisfactory conclusion without my intervention. When teaching kids about flexibility, the impulse to compromise should ideally emanate from within them, not the supervising adult. If there's going to be any flexibility, I want it to result from the kids' interactions, not from my desire for them to agree.

Key to the success of this exercise is that I am always perfectly willing to not go anywhere if the kids can't agree. This exercise is easier for me as a therapist than it might be for you as a parent: you may want so much for your child and his friend to be happy that you'd be unwilling to cancel the outing. But if you can bring yourself to hold firm, you will teach the invaluable lesson that, if you choose to remain rigid and refuse to compromise, you may not like the consequences. If you do end up canceling the outing, you have to be prepared to try again and go out another time.

Here's how things progressed:

    Me: So, where do you want to go?
Jimmy: I want to get ice cream.

> **Me:** And you, Adam?
> **Adam:** I want pizza.
> **Me:** Okay. You guys decide what to do and we'll go wherever you decide.
> **Both:** No, you decide!
> **Me:** I don't care. [And I really didn't.]

They went back and forth both, each one insisting that the other should go along with his own preference. They were at a stalemate. I needed to step in.

> **Me:** Well, in ten minutes, it'll be too late to go anywhere. [This was true.] So if you don't make a decision, we'll try again next week.

This would be fine. For this exercise, you need to be content to not go anywhere and give the children the opportunity to be more flexible.

Five minutes later:

> **Adam:** Okay, I'm fine with getting ice cream.
> **Jimmy:** Great. Let's go.

Now the therapy begins! The one thing I didn't do was prompt Jimmy to thank Adam for compromising. If I said, "Jimmy, what do you say?" or "Say thank you, Jimmy," the "thank you" would shut down the language exchange. It would be an etiquette lesson, not a therapeutic session. Instead, I continued:

> **Me:** Hold on, Jimmy. Adam really wanted to get pizza and

now he's willing to do what you want. What do you
think that means?

Jimmy: It means we're getting ice cream. Let's go!

Me: Yes, you're right, we are getting ice cream. But think
about it from Adam's point of view. He really wanted
pizza.

I waited and gave Jimmy time to think. Self-reflection is one of
the most important skills for children with autism to learn (neurotypical kids, too). All the exercises in this manual are geared toward
instilling this reflective process.

Jimmy: Okay. Next time we can get pizza. [A modest lesson
in flexibility has been learned.]

Me: That sounds fair. And you'll give up getting ice cream
next week?

Jimmy: Yeah.

Me: Whole sentence please, so I know what you're talking
about.

Jimmy: We'll have ice cream now.

Me: Because ...

Jimmy: Because Adam is being flexible, and next week we'll
have pizza and I'll be flexible.

Me: That may be hard, but you think you can do it?

Jimmy: Yes, it's fair.

Me (pushing it): And what will happen if Adam wants something
else, like Chinese food?

Jimmy: That'll be okay, too.

Me: What do you think of that idea, Adam?

Adam: Good!

They looked at each other and smiled. We left to get ice cream.

Accepting another person's feelings and differences.

I frequently have to assert my right to have feelings during a session. You—the parent, teacher, or therapist—have feelings, too, and no one can deny your feelings, not even an insistent, inconsiderate, obsessive, inflexible autistic kid who would like you to be just like him.

It's not unusual for clients to project their feelings onto me. Here's how it went with six-year-old Mike as we walked to the ice cream parlor.

> **Mike:** I want you to get coffee ice cream.
>
> **Me:** I know you love coffee ice cream, but that doesn't mean I have to get coffee ice cream.
>
> **Mike:** Yes, you have to get coffee ice cream.
>
> **Me:** I don't like coffee ice cream.
>
> **Mike:** Yes you do!
>
> **Me:** No, I don't. I DON'T LIKE COFFEE ICE CREAM. [I wasn't yelling; I was firm.]
>
> **Mike:** You do!
>
> **Me:** Listen, I know what I like. I like spaghetti. I like pizza. And I know what I don't like. I don't like olives. And I know that I DON'T LIKE COFFEE ICE CREAM.

Notice that I avoid the technique of asking Mike if he likes everything, the idea being that he might understand that I don't like some things just as he doesn't like some things. I avoid this because I don't want Mike to use himself as a reference. In this situation, I want him to accept my feelings because they're my feelings, not because we have something in common.

Me: Well, I'm not getting coffee ice cream because I don't like it.

Mike doesn't answer. He seems to have accepted my choice. We're almost at the ice cream parlor.

Me: I'm not getting coffee ice cream. Maybe I'll get chocolate, because I like chocolate ice cream.

Mike doesn't answer.

Me: (stirring the pot, because I know Mike loves coffee ice cream): Hey, why don't you get chocolate ice cream too? Then we can both have chocolate ice cream.

Mike: I'm getting coffee ice cream.

Me: I figured. And how about me?

Mike: You can get chocolate ice cream.

Me: Great! I love chocolate ice cream!

This conversation took a good twenty minutes. One small step for chocolate ice cream; one giant leap for being flexible and accepting another person's point of view.

OVERCOMING PERSEVERATION

Perseveration is the contin-
ual, involuntary repetition of
a thought or behavior. I once
worked with a child who would
continually suck the neckline of
his undershirt. Another would
wag his head back and forth, a
behavior popularly known as

stimming. Perseveration can manifest in speech, as when a child
repeats a syllable over and over, or in thinking, as when people
obsessively ruminate on a painful event.

Shuly, a nonspeaking eight-year-old, was perseverative in almost
everything he did: holding objects, walking, climbing, eating, jumping—once he started, he would continue the behavior until someone
interrupted him. I met Shuly many years ago when I was a counselor
at a camp for kids with special needs. Shuly's parents wanted me
to help him overcome his perseveration and become more flexible
in his thinking. I chose to focus on his eating habits, but any of
his other activities would have offered opportunities for flexibility
exercises, especially the activities that comforted him.

Shuly liked green peas. First he would eat all the peas on his
plate, and then he'd go around the table and eat the peas on everyone else's plate. Then he'd move on to the next thing he liked—say,
mashed potatoes—and polish off his own and then everyone else's.
To change this behavior, I put a small pile of peas on his plate with
a bit of mashed potatoes; that was all. Shuly ate a spoonful of peas;
then, before he could scoop up the rest, I thrust some mashed potatoes on his spoon. He resisted, but I knew he liked potatoes, so I

insisted. I was as insistent as he was resistant. You might say I was as stubborn as he was.

I remembered learning that, when feeding elderly persons who cannot feed themselves, you should rotate among the foods on the plate, just as you would do for yourself. I decided to use this technique with Shuly. And even though I didn't know how much language Shuly understood, I deliberately used appropriate language with him: "Now eat the potatoes… Okay, good. Let's switch now to the peas and after the peas, let's go back to the potatoes. Now you do it. Do it on your own. Switch. How about having something to drink and then going back to the potatoes? How about some chicken?" I was attempting to get Shuly to become more flexible, but also introducing a way he might better enjoy the contrasting tastes and textures of different foods.

Within a week, Shuly gained flexibility in his eating habits, which led to flexibility in other aspects of his life. Shuly felt he was controlling himself, perhaps for the first time, rather than being controlled by his perseverative impulses. He was more responsive to transitioning from one activity to another. To demonstrate to himself that he was controlling his functioning, he started asking to go to the bathroom rather than relieving himself in his pants.

The key here is that instead of insisting that the child stop a behavior, find another one that they like, distract them with the prospect of this new pleasure, and persuade them to partake of the new pleasure along with the old one. It goes without saying—but I'll say it anyway—that there are times when a child's perseverating must be stopped for safety reasons, such as when they're obsessively jumping near the rim of the Grand Canyon. But most perseverative behaviors are annoying rather than dangerous. Resist the impulse to halt the behavior, and tempt with other options instead.

WAITING TO TAKE TURNS

What does waiting mean? Waiting means you're paying attention to other people while they do something you'd like to do, because you understand that it's not your time to do it. Different people get to do the fun thing at different times. When it's your time to do it, it's your turn.

Learning to wait your turn is a skill that requires a person to be more flexible and less egocentric. The scene that follows depicts a therapeutic session that involved Ben, a nonspeaking three-year-old boy, myself, and a bag of popcorn.

> **Me:** Do you want some popcorn?
> **Ben:** (No response.)
> **Me:** (Offering him a kernel) Here's some popcorn.
> **Ben:** (Looks at the popcorn, takes it, and puts it in his mouth.)

Now it's my turn. I take a second kernel and hold it up between us. I bring the kernel up to my mouth, all the while observing Ben's body language: Is he watching what I'm doing or looking elsewhere?

Is he waiting for me to eat it? Is he watching me eat it? Is he preparing to grab it?

Observing the child's body language is crucial to see if their flexibility is evolving. Ben ate a kernel of popcorn; now I'm preparing to eat one. I'm watching closely to see how he's dealing with the idea that this next kernel is coming my way, not his.

Me: (with kernel in midair) This piece is for me.

If I start to put the kernel in my mouth and he grabs it from me, it's a sign that he needs to learn to be more flexible.

When you try this with your child, practice honing your powers of observation. As you take your turn and chew your kernel of popcorn, bite of cookie, or goldfish cracker, try to intuit whether your child understands that it's your turn now. Check his body language; watch what she does. Does he start to raise his hand to grab your piece, then stop himself when you indicate that this one is for you, not him? If he does stop himself, you can naturally intervene with language by asking, "Whose turn is it?" Does she reach for your piece and try to wrest it from you? If so, hold fast to your morsel and intervene with language: "This is my turn. Your turn comes next."

This exercise incorporates language, but its real purpose is to enhance flexibility. Inserting words into the process is secondary to introducing the concepts of waiting; healthy, controlled anticipation; and flexibility of mind and body.

OVERCOMING INFLEXIBILITY IN HIGHLY VERBAL CHILDREN/YOUNG ADULTS

Teaching flexibility to highly intelligent children and young adults.

Highly intelligent children and young adults on the spectrum can be deeply entrenched in their beliefs and loath to relinquish them. They sometimes have their own reasons for being inflexible, not the least

being their intellectual rigor and desire to know "the truth," however elusive it might be. Try as I may, I'm not always able to persuade a client to take a broader view when they've decided theirs is correct. In such cases, when I've reached the limits of my own authority, I seek out a higher one.

I once had a client who was convinced he had heart problems until I accompanied him to a cardiologist and sat with him as he underwent a battery of tests (his heart was fine). I took a young Jewish woman for a conference with a rabbi because she had questions that only God could answer and a rabbi was the closest person to God I could think of (if she'd been Catholic, I'd have found a priest for her to talk to; if she'd been Muslim, I'd have found an imam). I took a young man to an orthopedist because he'd convinced himself that he had developed shin splints after running half a mile. I brought an inventor to see a theoretical physicist who explained why the inventor's idea of a heated grid to prevent snow from sticking to sidewalks and driveways would not be cost-effective. And I took a young woman to a cardiologist because she had decided that her heart was literally cold, temperature-wise, and would cause her to die. The cardiologist pronounced her healthy, but she was still unconvinced, so I brought her to a yoga practitioner who had her lie on the floor and raise her legs over her head, causing her blood to rush toward her heart and persuading her that it wasn't cold after all.

These clients, all of whom were either kids or young adults, were prepared to accept the opinions of the experts I'd arranged for them to meet. I set up the excursions well in advance of the meetings, which the clients approached with trust and enthusiasm. This is a relatively easy way to encourage flexibility in folks who are still young enough to believe there are some people who know more than they do and that there may be a truth out there they can learn to accept.

But then there are those people who dismiss any and all information that comes from outside themselves. These can be the hardest nuts to crack, because their rigid shells prevent any new ideas from getting in.

My client Sam is a good example. Sam, eleven, is a devotee of a video game in which players mine terrain for raw materials and build a world of their liking. Sam's most beloved possession is Rusty, a virtual horse he jealously guards and won't allow to be ridden (names have been changed to protect the innocent). Too special for a stable, Rusty lives in a special house that Sam built for him and from which he is prevented from venturing because Sam is afraid someone will either harm or try to steal the horse. Living with Rusty is his son, a colt who doesn't yet have a name. In this dialogue, Sam and I are discussing Rusty's confinement.

Me: Do you ever take Rusty out for a ride?

Sam: Not anymore. I need to protect him. I like him so much, I don't want anything to happen to him.

Me: You're keeping him isolated because you like him so much, but that might not be good for a horse.

Sam: I don't care. He's my horse and I can do what I want with him.

Me: I know you love Rusty, but horses need exercise to keep healthy, just like people.

Sam: (After a pause) You're right, I should ride him more.

Me: How about letting my assistant take Rusty for a short ride? You've met her before, and she's ridden horses.

Sam: No.

Me: How about me? May I take him for a ride?

Sam: No.

Me: How about your mom?

Sam: No.

Me: Dad?

Sam: No.

Me: Your sister?

Sam: No way!

We were getting nowhere fast.

Then I had an idea. Another young client of mine, Lily, was about Sam's age and an enthusiast of the same game. With their mutual consent, I performed a virtual introduction, and they found that they enjoyed playing together. After a while, I contacted Lily and we came up with a strategy: she would ask Sam if she could ride Rusty's son while Sam rode Rusty, and then she would try to switch horses at some point during the session. She demonstrated her ability to care about Rusty while she rode Rusty's son. She asked

Rusty if he would like her to ride him and Rusty agreed. Excellent strategy: bypass Sam and go straight to the horse's mouth. Success!

Here is a lesson we already know: sometimes a peer has more influence than adults do. When I tried to cajole Sam into letting someone ride his virtual steed, he shut me down fast. But in the end, a friend persuaded him to loosen the reins. As much as we adults would like to gallop in and save the day, it's the kids who get to decide when and how they grow. We just need to guide them a little, often in the direction that they, not we, prefer. In this case, a computer game provided an opportunity for real as well as virtual interaction between Sam and a friend. This in turn pushed him to practice flexible thinking. He wasn't aware of it, which is all to the good: we often learn best when we're having fun.

CONCLUSION

All the exercises in this manual are designed to emanate either from an event initiated by the child or from an activity that interests the child. The guiding principle is simple: let the child lead, and when they do, be ready to follow.

Tune into the child's flow and create situations that foster natural growth. Each of us has moments of optimal experience; learn to identify these moments when they occur for your child, and use them to introduce language that expands the child's realm of expression. Taking your child on a fishing trip might yield memories that last for the rest of your lives, but don't stop there: use this engaging event to stage a potential breakthrough in your child's life. Any time your child is actively engaged with their surroundings is an opportunity for them to grow. Attune yourself to these moments and exploit them as best you can.

You must make the most of such moments because you never know when they'll occur and what riches they might yield. The hundredth time you repeat a phrase may be the one that nudges your child up to the next level. My client Jackie uttered his first word on a swing after literally years of silence. And there have been many other children whom I've witnessed making a quantum leap.

Myles was an eleven-year-old who had daily tantrums at school because he couldn't bear to be less than perfect. He despised his teacher, but he loved baseball. After half a dozen sessions in my office listening to Myles's near-encyclopedic knowledge of the game, I asked if he'd like to spend our next session outdoors, tossing around a baseball. He loved the idea.

The following week, I took him out to a baseball diamond, handed him a mitt, and started hitting pop flies in his direction. I noticed that Myles would twist his body away from the ball as it came toward him, moving to either side but never right under it. His catches, when he made them, were awkward and required more maneuvering and energy than were necessary. "Myles," I said, "I can show you an easier way to catch the ball. Want to see?" He nodded. I suggested he position himself directly under the ball and then tossed the ball upward and demonstrated a few times. Then I gently lobbed the ball in his direction, high enough to give him time to get under it. It worked: Myles began catching fly balls with ease.

And so it was that Myles stopped having tantrums after a single afternoon of baseball therapy. Lightning struck that day because Myles loved the sport: swinging a bat and sliding a mitt onto his hand were moments of optimal experience for him. He loved baseball so much that his desire to be better at it outweighed his shame at needing some coaching. After he mastered the catching technique, I explained that his teacher, with whom he was in constant conflict, was trying to help him, just as I was. "Yeah," he said, "but she's different from you. She says things in a different way." I asked him what he'd like her to say in order to help him. "I want her to say, 'I can show you an easier way for you to do that math problem, Myles,'" he said, using the same words I had used a few minutes earlier. I told him that made sense to me, and when I met with his teacher the following week, it made sense to her too. I coached her in how to speak to him, avoiding phrases that wouldn't bother a typical kid but that might trigger Myles's shame and anger. She called the next day to say she'd used the exact words Myles had suggested, and for the first time, he accepted her advice without getting riled. Their relationship changed, and the tantrums ended.*

---

* You can read more about Myles and other clients described here in *Uniquely Normal*.

Thirteen-year-old Jon was another kid who I thought might benefit from a session outdoors. Bombarded with sensory stimuli at home and at school, he was increasingly distractable and edgy. He was also grieving the death of his grandfather, who had been a source of consistent warmth and affection during his parents' recent divorce.

Jon was a bit of a rock hound—he dreamed of finding minerals within ordinary-looking stones—and said that he missed walking in the woods with his grandfather. "It's quiet in there," he said. "I like the way it makes me feel." I suggested we have a session in a nearby county park, and he was all for it.

The following week, I brought one of my son's old rock picks to the office, drove Jon to the park, and set out with him on a trail. Encountering a mammoth boulder with a seam of what looked like quartz running through it, Jon used the pick to extract a bit. He was ecstatic until a piece broke off.

I said, "You know, Jon, this little piece was once connected to your bigger one. How would you feel about letting me have it? If I keep it, we'll stay connected." His face lit up, and he handed me the fragment. To this day, I have that chip of quartz in a pouch in my office, along with fossils, pebbles, and the occasional geode I've found with other young people. They are tangible evidence of intangible moments of optimal experience, reminders of the redemptive power of paying attention to what my young clients are trying to tell me. When Jon said that he liked the way the woods made him feel, he was telling me that being in nature with his grandfather—who had been close to my age at the time of his death—comforted and healed him. I believe it is my mission, and yours, to be alert to the meaning encoded in your child's words.

Ten-year-old Andy's words didn't require decoding: he came right out and said he loved being outdoors. "I like trees, I like animals, I like dirt," he said. I understood why: trees, animals, and dirt didn't jeer at him, as the kids at school did. When Andy announced that he liked being in nature, I suggested we meet outdoors.

After an hour traipsing around the park, I showed up at our next session with a compass and a topographical map of the area. Andy knew what a compass and a map were, but he didn't know how to use them together. "See," I said, unfolding the map and positioning the compass on roughly the area where we were standing, "if we place the compass here, about where we are, it will show us which direction is north, and south, and east, and west." I gestured toward the sun, which had begun to decline into the treetops. "If you have a map and a compass, you can always know where you are. You'll never get lost."

Andy's mouth hung open; he was wonderstruck. I wasn't surprised: put a compass on a map and they become a magical thing. He took the map and compass from me and, holding them, pivoted slowly in a circle, watching the needle point steadily north no matter which direction he faced. His excitement was uncontained: he now possessed the knowhow to locate himself in the world. Disorientation is a fact of life for kids like Andy, who spend much of their lives trying to get their bearings in the neurotypical world. Now he had a way to orient himself in the woods—and, less literally, in the strange and sometimes savage jungle of school and social relationships. He was vibrating with pride when we parted and said he couldn't wait to tell his father what he'd learned.

When the COVID pandemic hit, Andy and I began meeting digitally. He'd share his screen with me while playing a video game, and I'd seize those moments to ask him concrete questions about what he was doing and why. Once, when he wanted to cut down a tree to build a deck on a virtual house, I asked, "You need an axe, but how are you going to get one?" He answered, "I have to dig up some ore and make one." "Okay," I said, "but what are you going to dig with?" "Oh," he said, "I'll go get a shovel." Immersed in the game, Andy wasn't aware that he was learning to express his thoughts in a cogent, logical way. I wasn't sure how effective these sessions were until the day Andy said, "I feel like we're walking in the woods." I took that to mean that he felt as comfortable and safe in our video habitat as he did outdoors.

Addison, an intelligent, energetic, highly distractable six-year-old, was wreaking havoc at school by flitting around the classroom, knocking pencils and papers on the floor and calling people names. She tried the same thing in my office, shoving and banging objects as she swept through the space. I was right behind her restoring order when I noticed lyricism amid the chaos: Addison was moving like a dancer, bending from the waist as she picked up a stuffed bear and daintily pointing her toes as she kicked it aloft. What first looked to me like random actions were actually Addison's moments of flow. When I commented on her grace, Addison said she loved to dance. But when I asked her to duplicate some of the movements she'd just performed, she couldn't: everything occurred spontaneously with no forethought or control.

For her next session, I arranged to have a yoga instructor in the room. Addison ignored her at first, then asked what yoga was, then performed a series of yoga poses along with her. The disciplined breathing of yoga imparted a steady rhythm to Addison's exertions; for perhaps the first time in her life, she was moving with intention and control. And she loved it: she learned that as she controlled her breathing, she could control her body and also her mind. Within a month, Addison's seemingly out-of-control behavior had almost disappeared.

Even though I hadn't predicted these breakthroughs, I was not surprised that they occurred. Each one originated in a child's moment of optimal experience, and because I was paying attention, I could identify and exploit it. My decades of working with children on the autism spectrum have equipped me to notice such moments, but your experience as a parent is equally valuable: no one knows your child as well as you do, and *no one is better qualified to help your child learn and grow*. If you make a conscious effort to go with the flow and keep in mind what would make a difference in your child's life, the right circumstances and opportunities will reveal themselves.

The ability to hone in on your child's needs in the midst of an organically engaging situation and identify the perfect intervention in that moment creates magic: like the perfect golf swing, it just feels right. And just like the perfect golf swing—or pirouette, piano solo, or soufflé—it takes patience and practice. That, and fifteen to twenty minutes a day. Have you got that much time to help your child?

I thought so.

ACKNOWLEDGMENTS

I would like to acknowledge the following people who helped make this manual possible.

Robin Cantor-Cooke, editor extraordinaire, extended herself to give me valuable input for this manual. Simply put, Robin is amazing!

Margaret Copely edited my work with diligence; she did not leave a stone unturned.

Sheila Hays, artist, musician, and poet, will struggle with me for hours figuring out whatever dilemma I may have. Day or night, she is there for me.

Howard L. Millman, a friend and an accomplished clinical psychologist, read every word of *Uniquely Normal* with love and care, and suggested writing this manual in the first place. I thought it was a good idea.

Simon Aronin always has the answers, if only I have the questions. Simon is a dear friend who helps in every aspect of my work.

Temple Grandin, after writing the foreword to my book *Uniquely Normal* commented on one aspect—that it is practical. That comment planted the seed for this manual, which is an even more practical hands-on guide. Thank you, Temple, for being right there, direct and honest.

And to the parents and children who always guide my practice: Thank you for keeping me learning and growing.

ABOUT THE AUTHOR

Robert J. Bernstein has devoted his career to improving the lives of children, teenagers, and adults with autism spectrum disorders. He developed his cognitive-based approach over more than thirty years of in-depth, one-on-one work with clients ranging from non-speaking toddlers to high-functioning adults. He is a consultant to the pediatric neurology departments at Bronx Lebanon Hospital; is an educational consultant to the National Council on Alcoholism and Other Drug Dependencies; has provided expert testimony at hearings on behalf of young people on the autism spectrum; and conducts evaluations for parents and health care providers. In addition to running his private practice, he conducts workshops, seminars, and support groups for families of persons with autism spectrum disorders and appears regularly on WVOX radio in New Rochelle. He is an active Board member of ARC and USAA and conducts monthly webinars for the USAA. Rob is an international lecturer and teacher trainer. He also founded the Table Tennis Therapy Program for Asperger's Individuals in Pleasantville, New York, the first program of its kind.

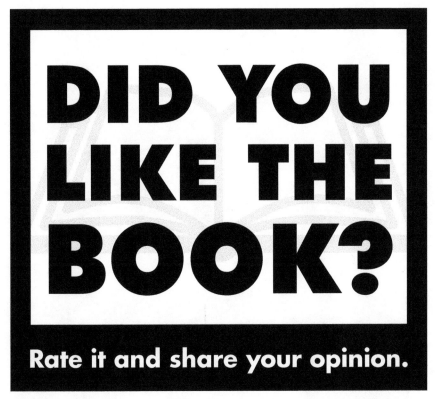

CPSIA information can be obtained
at www.ICGtesting.com
Printed in the USA
JSHW050314150123
36180JS00001B/1